Quotes for Lovers - And Others

by
James John Bianco

Edited by and Cover Design by:
Mrs. Linda Lee Bianco

AuthorHouse™
1663 Liberty Drive, Suite 200
Bloomington, IN 47403
www.authorhouse.com
Phone: 1-800-839-8640

First published by AuthorHouse 9/17/2007

ISBN: 978-1-4343-2897-7 (sc)

Printed in the United States of America
Bloomington, Indiana

This book is printed on acid-free paper.

This book is dedicated
in memory of:

Mr. Peter McWilliams

August 5,1949-June 14,2000

Peter McWillams was a Writer,Poet,as well as an Author, writting such books as,Catch Me With Your Smile,Love... And All The Other Verbs Of Life,Come Love With Me And Be My Life, as well as How to Survive The Loss Of Love to name just a few.

I never met Peter, but I believe if I had I believe we would of been great friends.

In troubled times of my own life, it was Peter

that helped me to go on when all seemed useless and dark.

After reading his book How To Survive The Loss Of Love, my life changed and, I began to notice things around me that I had never noticed before and, this is when I truely began to live.

Peter McWilliams was a gentle soul and, a man that inspired others to do amazing things. He made you look around and made you glad to be alive.

I truely believe if it were not for this man, I myself would not have been here today and, because of Peter I survived.

For those of you who would like to learn more

about this great man you can go to, Peter McWilliams on your computer.

All Through my life, my time of living I
have found that sometimes words,feelings,
as well as thoughts are sometimes if
not all the time,the hardest to speak of.
With the help of my friend I found
that each day that I grew I learned and,
as I learned I found that I gained knowledge
and, because no one ever stops learning
with each new day, I find I am still learning.
As I have said, words,feelings, as well
as thoughts are sometimes the hardest to
speak of and, the hardest to share and
because of this I now share them with you
so you the reader can share them with
others.
There's also something else I've
learned through the years and that is,
" today will be gone before you know it
and, tomorrow may never come and you may
never get another chance to tell someone
how you really feel or how much you'll
really miss them when their gone."

It seems every once in a while we argue, so lets
make it official, you go to your special room and,
I'll go to mine and, tomorrow we'll meet in the kitchen
and, I'll make you breakfast !

" I love you not only for who you are, but mostly
for what you have become to me "

" Loving you was easy, it was the waiting to find
you that was the hardest to do "

" I thought I knew what happiness was, until within
my life I found you "

" In a world filled with people, you and I found
that which is hardest to find... each other "

"The more I see you, the more I love you and, the
more I love you, the more I believe that without
you, I would be nothing "

1

" If I was granted only but one more day to live,
to love, I would spend it in search of you alone "

"Since I have come to love you, all else has become
unimportant and, the moments we have shared
more cherished than all the secrets untold that
wait before me "

" In all the days that I have spent within my time
of living, none shall ever compare to all those
that I have spent with you "

" Of all the brightest stars that I shall ever see,
none will ever be as brighter than your own
eyes that look deep within me and, help
my own to see "

" My dream is but a dream, my wish is but a wish,
but being with you here now, this moment is real,
giving me reason no longer to do neither "

" Lovers shall never be too young, nor too old,
for of age the heart knows not "

" Of all the sunsets I shall ever see, none shall
have more beauty, than when you share your love
with me "

" If it is true that the loss of love is the greatest
pain felt, rather than never love at all,
I shall welcome it "

" We've been together so long now, how about you marry me! I promise in the morning, I'll let you have the bathroom first ! "

" To never have loved , is to have never experienced
the second greatest gift given by God "

" Love is like seasons that come and go, but true
love lasts ....forever "

" Everyday being in love with you is like, a moment
in time I have as of yet experienced and, for this
my love will never grow cold "

" Living life without you isn't hard, living life
without you is my life's greatest tragedy "

" If I were to paint a portrait of my love for you,
it would be a masterpiece containing colors
never before used nor seen "

" Now that the parties over, these days I tend to
to find it more exciting having the same date
night after night and, taking home the same
lady as I have done at least hundreds of times
before "

" I love you so much that though in words it would be easy, to express it in paint on canvas, it would be hard finding one big enough to show what is truly in my heart "

" Fighting is easy having no rewards, but to find love and keep it, this alone is but a challenge with rewards of plenty "

" Without you, I am a star within an entire universe containing but one...myself "

" Getting use to you really isn't as important because I enjoy you, getting to know you is "

' It seems you've been with me mostly all of my life, but I'm not complaining, I'm just silently thanking God that you have been and, will always be so "

" To go to war, to fight and to kill simply to win,
somehow shall never seem more victorious
to me as is finding love,being loved, or to lie
in the closeness of another, to feel their warmth,
and be loved "

" You are the beauty of each new morning, with
hands like that of the rays of the sun that wakes me
with the touch of your softness, that allows me to
feel the warmth of each new day "

" You came to me and, like a snowflake so pure
yet ever so fragile, you alone taught me to be strong "

" Of all the greatest gifts God has given me, I have
always believed you were the best "

" Every night it's the same old thing, we make love and, talk for hours. How about tonight we just talk for hours and, then we'll make love ? "

" I've concidered what my world would be without you, but when I consider without you what the world would be, only then do I realize how truely lucky we are, you are here with us now..."

" As it is true that flowers and the leaves of trees grow and in time dry up and die only to return anew, then it shall be that we ourselves shall always like flowers and leaves...return "

" Like a ship sailing on the gentleness of waves, with your arms around me,your hands within my own, I know I am safe "

" The meaning of thinking of you is, something I enjoy doing when I am alone without you "

" If silence is golden, you and I must be millionare's
so here's a thought, why don't we pretend we're
poor for the next few hours"

" Though angel's come and angel's go, I am glad within my life you stayed "

" Do you believe in miracles? I do, each and every moment I spend looking at you "

" Within my life of living I have learned many things, mostly and importantly that, one can have all the money in the world, but without love, one is the poorest of all "

" Love is like a drug, though it may come and it may go, once accepted it is always needed and, without it one shall surely wilt and die in pain "

" They say, love is the most happiest the second
time around and, if this is so, what would you say,
if I asked you to marry me all over again ?"

" It is said, that money can't buy happiness and, I have in life found this to be true, but love... though to some is simply nothing, to others it brings the greatest riches of all "

" The love of a woman is the strongest human power of all known to man. It can be tender, it can be harsh. It can be warm or cold. It can make the weak gain strength, or take the strength from the strong "

" Love is the most dangerous drug of all, for it is a human emotion that has caused wars,death,deceipt and, even the fall of empires "

" In my time of living I have loved many and, felt within my pores and my soul the hurt and pain that love can bring. Oh how I long and look forward to love once again "

" Ok, your pregnant even though you say your
getting fat, but the truth is your not fat, your
pregnant and, this will be my first chance ever
to love two people at the same time. Maybe three,
maybe four or more ! "

" To live and die without having loved? I choose to live, to love and, to die, for have not to loved and died, is the sadest death of all "

" When you think about it, love can be many things such as, a cloud that carries you on it through softness, or drops you like a rock within the depths of the earth, a match that burns deeply or something that never visits at all. How I welcome the coming of love... "

" Love is like seasons, sometimes for some coming, for some going and for some one day returning, never to leave again "

" Life is but moments broken down into time, each being more precious than the other, each holding something new. Make sure you use them wisely, for in the next moment they could be gone forever "

" Hey, lets do it my way for a change, you sit down and watch football and, I'll do the cleaning and cooking "

" To find all the answers to all your questions of what I am within you, you must first look within yourself to find out who you truely are "

" Evil is the root of all that is, therefore it is better never to be planted "

" A face is a wonderful thing, for if put in it's right place it will always show you where you are going, not where you've been "

" God said, if you believe in me I will give you riches beyond your imagination, but though I am still without riches, with God I am the richest of all "

" Being blessed is not seeing what you believe, but believing in what you believe even though you do not see "

" It is always better to know where you are going, but sometimes it is made better to always remember where you've been "

" To try and to succeed is better than never to try
and succeed at nothing "

" God never said in life he would come to you, what
he did say is, that he would never let you walk
alone "

" I look around me and I wonder, why in a world
created so perfectly and beautiful, is there doubt..."

" Being a good friend, a husband, a wife or a parent
isn't easy, but just like a cake, what and how much
time you put into making it, makes it all the more
better "

" In teaching we teach, in listening we learn and, in
doing so we ourselves become better teachers "

" To know yourself is an accomplishment, but to have others allow you to get to know them, is a gift given only by a very special few "

" In an argument, getting the last word to you maybe
and acheivment, but sometimes listening can be
a greater one "

" Why is it that believing in unicorns and UFO's is so
easy, but believing in God is so hard ? "

" It seems at times I have an anti social personality
which stems from, I am only happy being with you "

" Only true words are spoken, when it is words truely
spoken from the heart "

" God may love all the rest, but you can bet among
all his best includes you "

" Looking at you all day long doesn't mean I am
obsessed with you, it simply means, knowing I
love you is also knowing without you in my life
I will never be able to love again "

" Knowing when to give up and surrender is the
wisdom of the weak, never doing so is the ability of
the strong "

" Beauty is a thing seen alone by the eye, but love
is but a feeling, seen by the heart "

" Art is beauty like that of a woman and, there are
collectors of many and collectors of one "

" Love can be beautiful or love can be ugly
depending on what one truely is within themselves "

" The words of a man have always been spoken,
yet the words of a woman are seldom heard, but
mostly right "

" Just now lying next to you I can hear the beating of your heart. What beautiful mucic it plays when we are alone lying in the closeness of each other "

" Wisdom does not only come with age, wisdom also come's with listening and thought "

" To scream,yell,holler,shout, always seems to lock the listening out "

" Life is but a sweet song and, with each new word, comes another note added to it's mucic "

" To feel, to touch,is the begining of all learning, listening is the best, but sometimes the hardest to do "

" To be young and grow, oh what an experience, but to be grown and to age and watch the young grow, oh what a wonder "

" Fathers and Mothers may scream and holler
alot at their children when they're bad,
but when you love someone, being quiet isn't
easy "

" Almost all fear dying, but it is better to have lived and died, than to never have lived at all "

" You may lose a friend because of love, but through love, you may find one "

" You may find a friend in a buddy, but you'll never find a best friend like dad "

" Nobody said loving your children would be easy, sometimes you just have too...
ground them "

" If you have to hit someone to make them understand...have someone else explain it "

" A good father is not someone who is always
like a furnace overheated, but in times of trouble,
one that always stays cool "

" Sometimes, words are the harshest punishment
of all and, sometimes are better left unsaid "

" To praise is to build, to ridicule is to condem
forever that which might of been made strong "

" Parents weren't always this smart, like our children
wisdom will come with age "

" Attention is sometimes far better than a single
word, a hug is even better and, with both you'll
never lose "

" How am I to be who I am, or what I am to be, if I
am to live in this world without you ? "

" There is no such thing as a bad child or a bad parent, but only the silent cry for help gone unnoticed "

" Living without you is like being in space
surrounded by millions of stars, yet still
alone in darkness "

" Lately I have been in a lot of pain, but my heart
is just going to have to realize your never
comming home and, start beating again "

" Falling in love with you when we first met was
easy and, now that we've been together for so
long I find falling in love with you again and again
much easier "

" When I was a boy I had everything, but when I
became a man and we met, it was then that
I realized that before you I had nothing "

" When you dream, dream from your heart, for it is in the heart alone where wishes are made "

" What I see within myself is real, yet what I see within you is impossible, but maybe thats because I've never really met anyone quite like you before during my time of being, of living, of loving "

" Changing who you are isn't easy, being exactly who you are and nothing more than is "

" Do not look to others for answers, for true answers try looking within one's self "

" To see with ones eyes is the abilty to see, to see from ones heart is a gift given to those who truely love others "

" When the time comes when my heart no longer
beats and, my body is laid in silent sleep, I shall
cherish most but my most fondest thought,
that in life I was loved by you "

" Never try being who you believe yourself to be, try being who you simply are, you "

" To resist the evil found in many, you must know who and what you truely are within your self "

" What's amazing to me is that so many people talk about finding true love, but yet so many never stay together long enough to find out "

" Finding and loving someone will never be as harder as getting to know that someone when you do "

" When in love as in death, when they come all will be perfect "

" To love someone is to be willing to give your
own life so they may live and continue to go
on even though you have passed on "

" Of all the greatest gifts that I have ever received, you are the best and, your love the greatest of all "

" Loving someone is loving them for who they are, not for what you believe them to be "

" My life has become like that of a dictionary and, I have found myself searching for words and phrases, to express what I feel within my own life for your own "

" True friends will always stay, but when your down you'll find the one's who are, will seldom stray "

" With a good heart one never needs to fear that which lies before you "

" The short road is always the easiest however, the long road is sometimes more fulfilling and, sometimes the hardest choise to make "

" If your going forward never look back, for looking back sometimes only makes the journey that much longer "

" Women come and women go, but they'll never be a woman quite like mom "

" Letting someone go that you love is the hardest action of one's heart. Having that person return, is the action of true love "

" To love and surrender to love, is but to follow one's heart, to stay and to love forever is the surrender of both "

" Do not allow the shadows of your heart to hinder what the heart will feel oneday again "

" Love knows no color,no race, for it is love alone
that the heart searches for, finds and, holds
closest "

" Without love there can be no friends,no lovers and, no feelings to fill the room of an empty heart "

" To love is to love, but to love being in love and to be loved in return, is to know you are alive "

" Love is a gift given to another that comes from the heart of one who gives "

" Depending on love alone without ever trusting is to depend on something without ever believing "

" There are those who live and love and are remembered and, those who live and love only to feel alive "

" Love can be as strong as a trunk of an oak, or
as weak as a pedal of a rose, depending on
how much care is taken in growing it "

" To love is to love one for who they are and, what
they are within themselves not, what and who
you wish them to be "

" If you have to ask if your loved, what you have
is not love but a friendship, but with patience
only the heart will tell "

" Depending on how much water is given all plants
will grow, as it is true with the heart depending on
how much love is given, will depend on what you
will get in return "

" To love someone never knowing if love will be
returned is a chance, to receive it back, is a gift "

" Dreams are wishes that are created in the heart
of those who love and, there are those who wish to
be loved, but find love only in dreams "

" There are those who have died in love, for love and, those who have died without living at all. Though I dread the thought of dying, I dread more,the dying without having ever experienced both "

" May you always live to dream and to love "

The Author

James John Bianco

www.ingramcontent.com/pod-product-compliance
Lightning Source LLC
Chambersburg PA
CBHW021303280526
45784CB00005B/2491

* 9 781434 328977 *